Orienteering

Neil
Champion

WAYLAND

First published in 2008 by Wayland

Copyright © Wayland 2008

Wayland
338 Euston Road
London NW1 3BH

Wayland Australia
Level 17/207 Kent Street
Sydney NSW 2000

Senior editor: Jennifer Schofield
Designer: Rachel Hamdi and Holly Fulbrook
Photographer: John Cleare – www.mountaincamera.com
Proofreader: Susie Brooks

Acknowledgements:
The author and publisher would like to thank Christine Robinson
at British Orienteering and all those who helped with the photoshoot.

All photography by John Cleare except
5 left Klein J.L. & Hubert M.L. /Still; 28 top and 29 Mikko
Stigg/Reuters/Action Images,
28 bottom Reuters/Action Images

British Library Cataloguing in Publication Data
 Champion, Neil
   Orienteering. - (Get outdoors)
   1. Orienteering - Juvenile literature
   I. Title
   796.5'8

ISBN: 978-0-7502-5059-7

Printed in China

Wayland is a division of Hachette Children's Books,
an Hachette Livre UK company.
www.hachettelivre.co.uk

Note to parents
and teachers:
The website addresses (URLs)
included in this book were
valid at the time of going
to press. However, because
of the nature of the Internet,
it is possible that some
addresses may have
changed, or sites may have
changed or closed down
since publication. While the
Author and Publishers regret
any inconvenience this may
cause the readers, no
responsibility for any such
changes can be accepted
by either the Author or
the Publisher.

Disclaimer:
In preparation of this book,
all due care has been
exercised with regarad to
the advice, activities and
techniques depicted. The
Publishers regret that they
can accept no liability for any
loss or injury sustained. When
learning a new sport, it is
important to get expert
tuition and to follow a
manufacturer's advice.

Contents

What is orienteering?

Orienteering involves finding your way around a set course using a map. You go from one fixed marker (called a control point) to another, until you reach the end of the course. The courses are found in a variety of places in the outdoors and they range from about 2 kilometres to 15 kilometres in length.

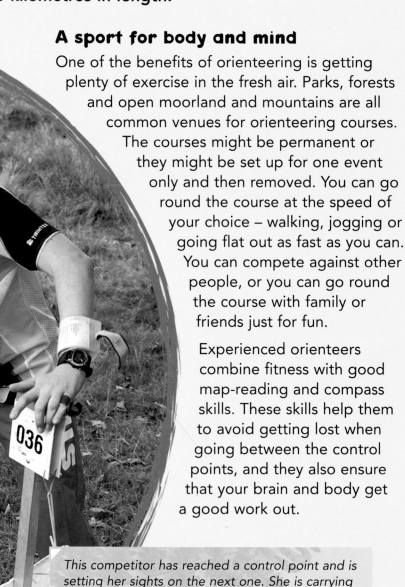

A sport for body and mind

One of the benefits of orienteering is getting plenty of exercise in the fresh air. Parks, forests and open moorland and mountains are all common venues for orienteering courses. The courses might be permanent or they might be set up for one event only and then removed. You can go round the course at the speed of your choice – walking, jogging or going flat out as fast as you can. You can compete against other people, or you can go round the course with family or friends just for fun.

Experienced orienteers combine fitness with good map-reading and compass skills. These skills help them to avoid getting lost when going between the control points, and they also ensure that your brain and body get a good work out.

This competitor has reached a control point and is setting her sights on the next one. She is carrying her map and compass in her right hand.

The roots of the sport

Orienteering started in Sweden in the first decade of the twentieth century. The first competition took place there in 1918. Orienteering was seen as a sport that needed little complicated equipment and so could be taken up by just about anyone. As it was set in the countryside, the cost of taking part was very low. From Sweden, the sport has spread all over the world and today it is a truly international sport. The first world championship was held in 1966 and now this event happens every year, with participants coming from countries including Kazakhstan, Moldovia, USA, Great Britain, Australia and New Zealand.

These two photographs show two types of orienteering – getting around by bike and the more traditional running. Different types of orienteering have helped the sport to grow.

How to get started

Orienteering is an easy sport to take up. There are permanent courses set up that anyone can use, and the best way to get started is to find one of these courses near you.

Permanent orienteering courses (POCs)

There are around 150 permanent courses in Britain alone and many more in other countries around the world. These have been designed with beginners in mind. Because the courses are permanent, you can go along and use them whenever you want. All you will need is a special orienteering map of the course. Orienteering maps show all the control points and the type of countryside you will be running through. They have been designed so that you can easily identify things such as dense woodland and scrub, which is best avoided because it will be difficult to get through, or open woodland, which is easier to run through. Often a local orienteering club will have a 'map pack' that will list all permanent courses in your area.

These young children are studying the map of a POC together before setting off.

Permanent course maps and colour-coded courses

Permanent course maps will have a large scale – maybe 1:5 000 or 1:10 000 (see page 13). A red triangle on the map marks the start of the course. The maps will also have red circles marked on them to indicate where the control points can be found. The control points will often be a post near a path in a wood, in the undergrowth or beside a stream. You can make your own way from one control point to another using a compass, or you can follow a marked course that will be colour coded, depending upon the difficulty. The colour-codes are:

White – *these courses are usually about 2 kilometres long. They are the easiest courses and usually have about six control points. They are ideal for beginners.*

Yellow – *these courses can be up to 3 kilometres long. The control points will be harder to find, but they are still suitable for beginners.*

Orange – *these courses are longer (4–5 kilometres) and control points are harder to locate.*

In addition to these colours you will find red, green, blue and brown courses, which are all longer and harder and suitable for more experienced orienteers.

Joining a club

Once you have navigated yourself around POCs and you would like to orienteer more often, you could join a local club. To find your nearest club, you can contact your country's national governing body, for example Orienteering Australia or the US Orienteering Federation in the USA. Clubs organise both training and competition events, in which you can participate. Competitions are usually divided into different age groups for men and women and also into different categories of difficulty.

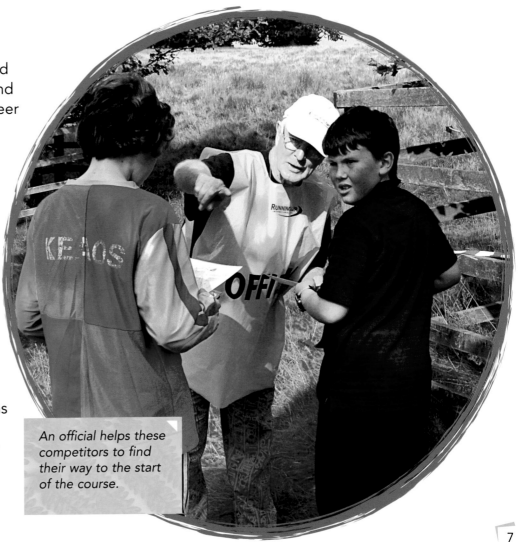

An official helps these competitors to find their way to the start of the course.

A sport for all

Whatever your age or fitness or ability, there will almost certainly be an orienteering course that you can do. Clubs cater for all age groups, from under 10 to over 70 years. These age classes are also separated into men's and women's events. Also, schools and organisations, such as the Scouts and Guides, often organise orienteering events for their members.

Joining in

It does not cost very much to join a club and get started. Often, you can borrow more expensive equipment – for example, a compass or map – from the club. Do not forget, orienteering is not just for fast, athletic people. It is just as important to use your brain and plot the best course through all the control points to the finish. By joining a club you will meet other more experienced orienteers, who will be able to give you tips and hints on how to go around courses.

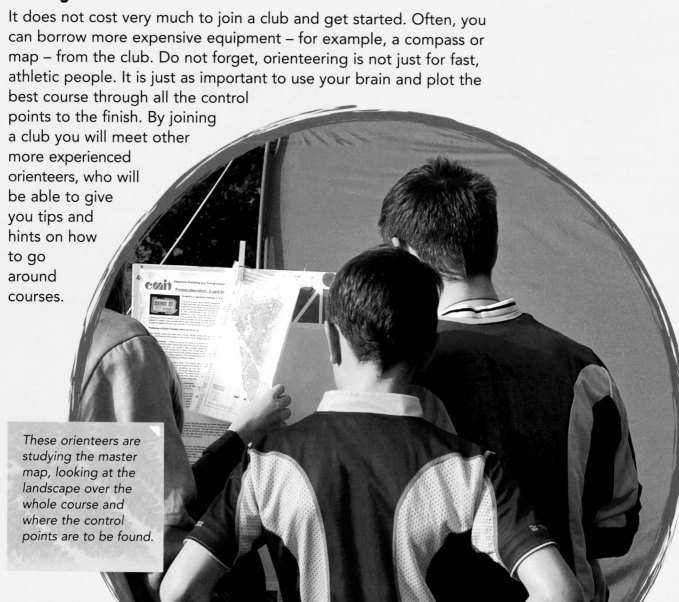

These orienteers are studying the master map, looking at the landscape over the whole course and where the control points are to be found.

Types of orienteering

There are four main types of orienteering. Orienteering on foot, whether walking or running, is known as Foot-O. This is the most popular kind of orienteering. Courses can also be done on skis (known as Ski-O) in regions where there is plenty of snow, such as Scandinavia. There are also courses for mountain bikes (called MTB-O) and wheelchairs (called Trail-O).

Disabilities

There are very few real barriers to taking part, for fun or in a competition. Trail-O courses have good surfaces for wheelchairs. Trail-O events demand exactly the same skills as any other course – fitness, navigational skills and a sense of fun and adventure – but the emphasis is on difficult navigation rather than speed. This means that able-bodied and disabled orienteerers can compete on equal terms.

A good way to get started in orienteering is through your school, where teachers can help you learn the basics.

The Age Classes

Usually competitions are divided into different age groups and these are then divided into male and female competitors:

Under 10 years

11 and 12 years

13 and 14 years

15 and 16 years

17 and 18 years

19 and 20 years

21 to 34 years

35 to 39 years

40 to 44 years

45 to 49 years

50 to 54 years

55 to 59 years

60 to 64 years

65 to 69 years

70 years and older

Orienteering equipment

One of the advantages of orienteering is that you do not need a lot of equipment to start taking part in events. However, because the sport takes place in the countryside at all times of year, you will need to think about the weather and what type of clothing you should wear.

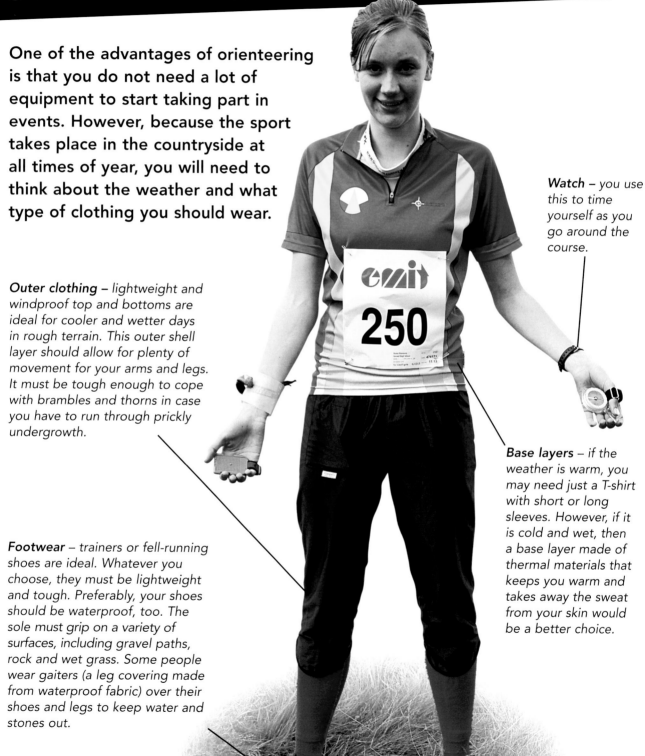

Watch – you use this to time yourself as you go around the course.

Outer clothing – lightweight and windproof top and bottoms are ideal for cooler and wetter days in rough terrain. This outer shell layer should allow for plenty of movement for your arms and legs. It must be tough enough to cope with brambles and thorns in case you have to run through prickly undergrowth.

Base layers – if the weather is warm, you may need just a T-shirt with short or long sleeves. However, if it is cold and wet, then a base layer made of thermal materials that keeps you warm and takes away the sweat from your skin would be a better choice.

Footwear – trainers or fell-running shoes are ideal. Whatever you choose, they must be lightweight and tough. Preferably, your shoes should be waterproof, too. The sole must grip on a variety of surfaces, including gravel paths, rock and wet grass. Some people wear gaiters (a leg covering made from waterproof fabric) over their shoes and legs to keep water and stones out.

Map – an orienteering map shows the start of your course, all the control points and the finish. Do not forget a waterproof cover in case of rainy weather.

Compass – this should be a magnetic compass that is lightweight.

Red pen – this is used to mark your course on your map, to help you make decisions once you have started.

Whistle – like a first aid kit, this is a piece of emergency gear that might be important on longer mountain courses.

Being Weather-Wise

Remember that weather can change. A hot, sunny start to an event might end in rain and wind. Make sure you check the weather forecast for the area where you will be orienteering, then take the right clothing to cope with the conditions. This means keeping cool when the temperature is high, and staying warm when the wind is blowing and the sun goes behind clouds. Orienteering takes place all year round, so think how cold it can get in the middle of winter.

Brikke – (pronounced brick) this keeps a digital record of each control point you have visited.

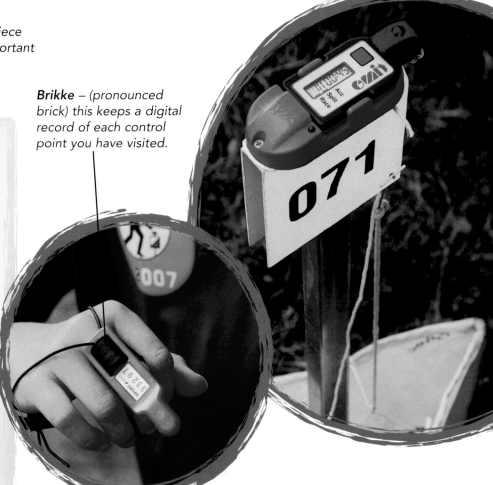

Work Rate and Temperature

Do not forget that the harder you intend to run, the warmer you will be. So make sure your clothing suits not only the weather conditions, but also your own running rate. For example, on a cool and windy day, you may need only shorts and a T-shirt if you intend to run the entire course. If you walk the whole course, you might want to wear a windproof top and tracksuit bottoms as you will not be generating that much heat from your effort or work rate.

Understanding the map

Being able to understand and read the course map accurately is the most important skill you will need to learn as an orienteer. If you find it difficult, do not be put off – once you start using maps, you will become more familiar with them and soon reading the map will be second nature to you.

On the map

Navigation is impossible without the map. The map contains all the information you will need about the course – its length, the type of terrain you will come across, where the control points are positioned, the start and finish marks, hazards to avoid and clues to help you find your way around. It will also help you to make crucial decisions about which route to take between control points – the shortest path but over the toughest ground or the longer way on better trails? The choice is yours, but only if you know how to read the map.

It is important to be able to relate the landscape you can see with the map of the course you will be running around.

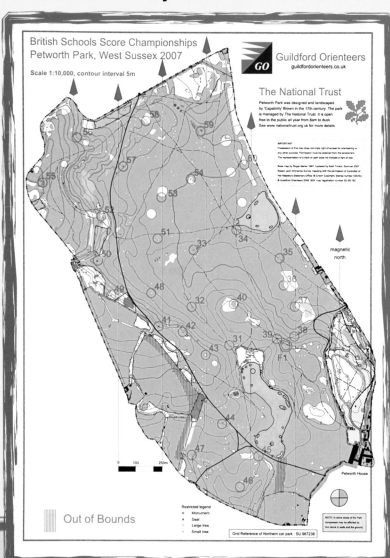

Reading Symbols

Colour	What it means
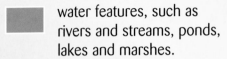	water features, such as rivers and streams, ponds, lakes and marshes.
	mostly man-made features, such as roads and paths, fences and walls, railway lines and buildings. However, rocky ground (cliffs and outcrops) is also shown in black.
	land features, the most important being contour lines. These lines show the height and the shape of the landscape.
	type of vegetation. Most importantly, this shows how how dense or open the vegetation is, indicating if you can run quickly over it or whether you will have to fight your way through it.
	land use and vegetation type, in open land such as fields and moorland.
	open woodland.

To use your map in conjunction with your compass, keep your thumb over the point to which you are headed.

Reading the signs

To understand the map, you will need to be able to 'read' the special language it uses. This is the visual language of signs, shapes, colours, land and water features as well as the scale and the concept of magnetic north. The red triangle shows the start of the course and the red double circle shows where the finish is. The single circles show the control points that you will have to find to be successful. To find these points you need to be familiar with the coloured symbols on the left.

Scale

Most orienteering maps are 1:10 000 or 1:15 000 in scale. On 1:10 000 maps, every centimetre you measure on your map represents 100 metres on the ground. When you are given your map, measure in centimetres how far it is from the start of the course to the first control point. You then need to work out how far this is in reality. To do this, multiply the centimetres by either 100 or 150, depending on the scale of your map. For example, if the scale is 1:10 000 and you measure 3 centimetres from the start to the first control point, you multiply this by 100. The distance you need to cover is 300 metres.

Magnetic north

All magnetic compasses used in the northern hemisphere point to magnetic north. The top of your map is aligned to magnetic north, too. You will find straight lines on your map going from top to bottom. These are grid lines and point north (top) and south (bottom). Some maps have lines that point to grid north rather than magnetic north. In this case, you will have to make allowance for the difference by adjusting your compass.

Using a compass

To use the map to its full potential, you need to be able to use a compass. The compass will help you to set the map and take a bearing to find your next control point.

A navigational tool

There are different compasses available, including thumb compasses. These are used by experienced orienteers who need to run very fast and have a compass to hand at all times. The compass shown here is a standard type used by walkers and is suitable for general navigation and orienteering.

Use your compass to orientate the map, lining up north (the top of the map) with magnetic north (shown by the red needle of the compass).

Setting the map

The red end of the movable magnetic needle always points to magnetic north. To set the map (arrange it so that it faces the same way as the features in the real world), all you need to do is place the compass on top of it and align the map grid lines with the magnetic needle. Make sure the north (red) end of the needle faces towards the top (north) end of the map. Now look at the features on the map and find them in the landscape around and in front of you. Being able to set the map is a very useful skill – especially when visibility is poor, you are lost, or the landscape is very flat and featureless.

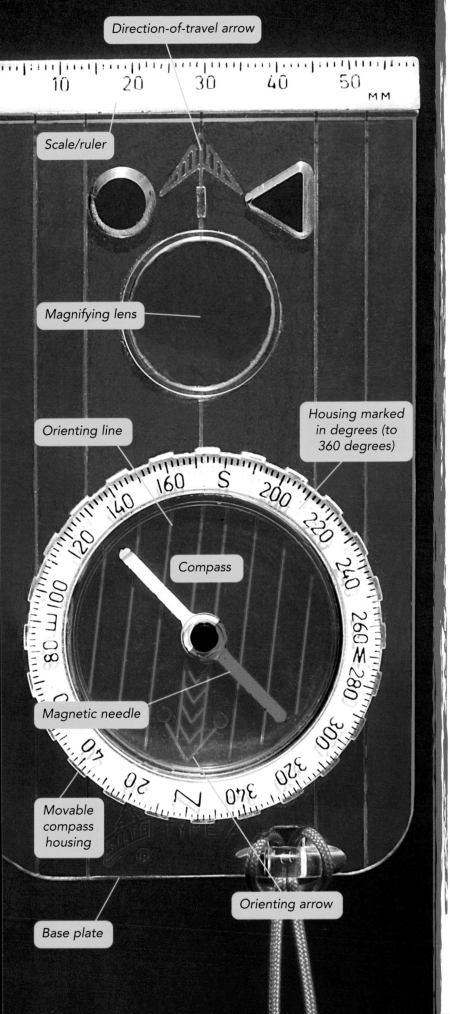

Direction-of-travel arrow

Scale/ruler

Magnifying lens

Orienting line

Housing marked in degrees (to 360 degrees)

Compass

Magnetic needle

Movable compass housing

Base plate

Orienting arrow

Taking a bearing

You can use the map and compass to find the direction between you and the thing you are trying to get to, such as a control point. The direction, or bearing is usually given in degrees (between 1 and 360). These are read off from the compass housing.

1. Put the edge of the compass on the point on the map that shows where you are standing. Line up the compass with the place you want to reach (for example a control point).

2. Turn the compass housing so that the orienting lines match up with the grid lines on the map (make sure the north-south lines face the same way).

3. Take the compass off the map and swing the magnetic needle around so that it lies on top of the orienting lines, with both red ends of the arrows facing the same way (north).

4. Read the compass where the line of the direction-of-travel arrow touches the housing of the compass marked off in degrees. This is your bearing.

5. If you hold the compass in front of you and keep the magnetic needle over the orienting lines, you can walk to the control point using the direction-of-travel arrow as your guide.

Training body and mind

To be good at orienteering, you have to combine physical fitness with mental agility. The sport is not simply about going from one control point to another as fast as you can. It is also about making navigational decisions based on reading the map.

Doing high kicks to touch your hand will warm up your legs. Do this gently and remember to use both legs in turn.

Running gently on the spot is a good way to warm up before a competition.

Warming up

Before an orienteering event, it is a good idea to warm up your muscles. Try to develop a routine in which you jog or skip gently on the spot to make your heart beat a little faster. This will send blood to your muscles and signals to your brain that you are about to take physical exercise. In doing this, you should avoid straining yourself in a competition. Avoiding injury is the main aim of warming up, but warming up also helps your body to perform better.

Stretching

Stretches need to be done carefully and only after you have warmed up or at the end of an event. Strenuous exercise can lead to stiff muscles and sore tendons, and stretching helps to prevent this. When you stretch, make sure you hold your stretches for at least 10 seconds and do not push too hard. If your muscles feel like they are about to snap, you are over-stretching them and will injure yourself.

Mental training

When navigating, you will need to find the quickest route possible. This is not always the shortest – for example, if the map tells you that the shortest route leads you through dense undergrowth. Taking a longer path through easier ground might end up being the best choice. Training your mind to make quick decisions and then asking your body to carry them out is what orienteering is all about. To prepare your brain for the mental calculations of measuring distance, taking bearings and reading the map, you will need to take part in lots of orienteering challenges. Only by doing the sport will you be able to improve. You will also have to get used to moving fast whilst carrying and using the map and compass.

Staying Focused

It is important to stay focused. This means keeping mentally alert while you tackle the course. You will have to stay in contact with the map at all times, knowing your position and the point you are aiming for. At the same time, you need to keep an eye on the landscape you are running through. Does it correspond to the map? Are you taking the best line from one point to another? What type of terrain is coming up on the horizon? You need to keep thinking about all this information while you are on the go.

Stretches like these will benefit you most after you have been running and should be used as a warm-down routine.

Developing your skills

Orienteering combines mental and physical strengths. Both are needed to succeed in this sport. For example, you need to be able to calculate distance and your speed and take bearings with your compass. You then need to have the fitness to run along that bearing to reach your destination.

Visualising the map

Before setting off on any orienteering course, whether for fun or in a competition, it is important that you study the map and the course marked on it. The map will tell you the overall length of the course, the distances between the control points, and how many control points you need to find. It will also tell you where the finishing point is. You must look more closely at the signs and symbols to find out what the vegetation cover on the ground will be like and what the contours tell you about the shape and height of the landscape. Is there thick woodland or undergrowth to avoid? Is there a big hill you can go around rather than slog up and over? Is there treacherous marshy ground to pick a way through?

If you study the map carefully, there should be few surprises along the route once you start. Experienced orienteers carry this information in their heads as they run the course. This way they can tick off features they have remembered from the map that will tell them they are going in the right direction. Remember, this does not come easily to most people. You will need to get out there and practise to become any good at it.

Just before setting off on the course, these orienteers are trying to visualise the map features and memorise them.

Estimating distance and speed

As you become more experienced, you will become more accurate at judging distances. Using the map, you can accurately measure how far you have to go from one point to another. Remember, different-scaled maps have different measurements, so make sure you know which scale map you are using. When you have worked out how far you have to go, you should be able to estimate that distance on the ground beneath your feet. One of the ways to do this is to be able to judge how far you have travelled using timing (you will need to know roughly how fast you are going to do this) and another is by using pacing (see panel on right).

Accurate timing

Most people walk at about 3 kilometres per hour. This means that they will cover 100 metres every two minutes. However, you might be walking at a fast pace of 6 kilometres per hour when you orienteer, in which case you would cover 100 metres in one minute. If you started to jog slowly, you might be going at 8 kilometres per hour or 45 seconds per 100 metres. The trick is to know how fast you are walking or running. You can then estimate how long it will take you to reach your control point (once you have measured the distance on your map, that is).

To use pacing and timing accurately, you will need to practise running over a measured distance of 100 metres.

Accurate Pacing

Another way to measure your distance is to pace it. To do this, you will need to accurately measure 100 metres on the ground. Then walk this distance, counting every double pace you take until you reach the finishing mark. Do this again to check your count. Most people walk 100 metres in about 65–70 double paces. Memorise your double paces for this distance at a fast walk and a gentle run. In this way, you can estimate how many double paces it should take you to cover any distance on the ground between one point and another and you will know how long the course should take you.

Orienteering techniques

Once you have mastered the basic skills of using a map and compass and estimating distance on the ground using timing and pacing, you can move on to some of the techniques used in navigating. Remember, the more you try, the better you will become at using these techniques.

Handrails

Handrails are features on the landscape and on the map that make a line that you can follow. They include fences, paths, streams or rivers and walls. Use them as much as possible if they lead you in the right direction. If you are lucky, they will take you right to your destination. However, if they do not, then note carefully on the map where you should leave them to strike out on a bearing (see page 15) to finish off your leg.

Using the fence as a handrail will give you a line to follow.

Features such as woodland provide a point to aim off towards.

The point where two paths meet is an obvious attack point to use.

Aiming off

Aiming off is a technique often used together with a handrail feature. If your control point is somewhere along a river, you could take a bearing from where you are to where it is, and follow that bearing. However, if you are slightly out when you arrive at the river, you might not know whether to turn left or right to find the control. You might waste valuable time going the wrong way. If you deliberately take a bearing to one side or the other of the control point, when you arrive at the river you will know which way to turn. This is called aiming off.

Attack points

You can use an obvious feature that is easy to find as an attack point, before tackling a trickier piece of navigation to find your control point. An attack point might be where a path changes direction, where a wall suddenly stops, or where two streams meet. It has to be something that you could not fail to find. You should be able to run to it quickly, without much or any reference to the map.

When something goes wrong

The aim of every person tackling an orienteering course is to know where they are on the map and on the ground at all times. The skills needed to be able to do this include good map interpretation, being able to recognise landscape features, judging distances, following compass bearings, and the ability to make decisions about which line to follow.

Getting lost

Everyone gets lost at some point. The most important thing is not to panic and to relocate yourself as quickly as you can. On a local course there will be plenty of people in the area and probably buildings and roads close by, so there should be no real danger in the situation. However, if you take part in an event in more remote countryside (on moorland or in the mountains, for example), getting lost can be more serious. Even then you should stay calm. The event organisers will have plans in place to help people and you should have information on this before you set off.

This orienteer is lost. However, by studying the map closely and thinking of his last known point, he should be able to work out where he is.

Emergency!

In the event of an emergency, you should know what to do. Carrying a whistle to attract attention is a good idea. A whistle can be heard much farther away than a person shouting. The international signal to get help in the mountains is six blasts on the whistle, then an interval of one minute. Then keep repeating the six blasts and the minute silence until aid comes. If you hear three blasts on a whistle, that means that someone has heard you and help is on the way.

If you need to attract attention, use your whistle to call for help.

Coping with injury and illness

Occasionally orienteers are injured or feel ill. The most common injuries affect the legs – a twisted ankle or a painful knee or hip. Other injuries include insect bites, vegetation scratches and getting something in an eye. Illness can come on suddenly. Over-exertion, sunstroke, dehydration, and hypothermia are all conditions to watch out for. If something happens to you or you find someone suffering an injury or illness, then make sure you stop. Getting help to you is the most important thing. Remember, if you have asthma, diabetes or any other illness for which you need to take medcine regularly, make sure you take it along with you.

Relocation

If you find yourself in countryside that you do not recognise from the map, stop immediately. To carry on blindly in the hope that you will find a clue to your whereabouts is not a good idea. Try to remember the landscape you have been travelling through. What vegetation was there? Was it hilly or flat? What prominent features did you pass (a stream, a path or a wall)? Now look closely at your map. Where was the last place at which you knew where you were? Look for the things you have just remembered. Can you find them on the map? If you were running on a bearing, look back along the line you have run along (called a back bearing). Can you pick up on where you might have gone wrong? You are probably not far off your course, so think logically about where you want to be and where you actually are. Do not rush this process of relocating yourself.

At competitions there should be a first aid kit available for any injuries or medical emergencies.

Competitive orienteering

Taking part in a competition is great fun. It will test all aspects of your orienteering skills – fitness, decision-making, and navigating. Events are colour-coded to suit all levels of ability (see page 7) and they will have age classes, too.

Using the Controls

In the past, a clipper or punch with a unique pattern of pins was used to mark a control card. Today, an electronic system is used. The system uses a brikke (see page 11), which is carried by each competitor and can be electronically 'punched' at each control, recording your visit. Once you have recorded your visit by using either system, you will be ready to move on to find the next control. Do not forget that you not only have to find each control, but you must also find the controls in the correct order.

When you arrive at a competition, collect your map as soon as possible so that you can study it against the master map.

Getting ready

Once registered with the organisers, make sure you know your starting time and have your map. Copy the course information from the master map onto your map with a red pen. Give yourself a little time to study your map and work out how you will get around all the control points to the finish. Also, you may want to do some simple warming up exercises to prepare your body as well as your mind for the test ahead.

Arriving at a control point

Control points are marked on the map. The skill of an orienteer is to read the landscape as it is shown on the map, to pick the quickest route from one control point to another and then to actually carry out that plan. When you arrive at a control point, you will find a red-and-white triangle (or red-and-white post). It will have a unique code to distinguish it from all other controls. This will be either in the form of a clipper with which you will mark your card, or it will be electronic and used together with a brikke that you will be carrying with you.

Finishing the course

The last point you have to find is the finish. When you reach the finish, make sure you report to the organisers. This helps them to ensure that everyone has returned safely. It also gives you a time for your finish and proof of your successfully having been to all the control points along the way. Now you just have to wait to find out how well you did compared to the other people on your course and in your age class.

At the end of a gruelling competition, you may need to run flat out to finish with a good time.

Designing a course

A lot of thought goes into planning an orienteering course. The level of the course (what level of ability the designer is aiming for), whether it is for those with disabilities or not, the overall length, the difficulty of navigation, safety – all these things have to be taken into consideration. It is useful for you to understand some of these factors that the people who make orienteering courses have to keep in mind. You might even want to have a go at designing your own course on paper.

Some of the basics

One of the first things course designers think about is where the course can be laid out. This will depend upon a number of factors, such as who owns the land and what type of land is it – for example, is it parkland, open woodland or upland moors? Course designers also need to think about the safety of the orienteers – for example, is there a fast-flowing, deep river on the site, or marshy ground in which people could become stuck?

Open woodland paths provide easy ground for competitors to run through.

Designers also need to think about how difficult the course's navigation should be to fit the levels of event that are going to be held on it. This is especially hard if there are beginners as well as more experienced orienteers.

The different levels

There are eight different colour-designated levels of difficulty in orienteering. These go from white, which is the easiest, to brown, which is the hardest (see page 7). Different types of country will suit the different levels, and course designers need to take this into account.

Local and easily accessed parks will make good venues for the easier, white, courses. Moorland, mountains and woodland are more remote and the landscapes are more varied and difficult, so they make better courses at the harder levels. This means it is challenging for organisers of events to ensure that all levels are catered for, so do check which levels feature in a competition before you enter.

Dense forest makes it harder for competitors to look for the control points.

Open grassland makes it easier for an orienteer to scan the countryside looking for clues as to where the next control point is located.

Orienteering around the world

Orienteering is a sport that can be organised and run in a wide variety of landscapes. Courses can be laid out in deserts, mountains, forests, parkland, and areas of mixed hill and lowland. It is therefore no wonder that the sport has become popular in many countries around the world.

France's Thierry Gueorgiou takes part in the 2007 world championship.

A world sport

Orienteering is a truly international sport. It has always been very popular in Sweden, where it started, Norway, Denmark and Finland. The sport spread from these Scandinavian countries to other countries such as Russia, Hungary and Switzerland, and then to the rest of Europe and the USA. Countries as far flung as Japan, Australia, and New Zealand are today members of the International Orienteering Federation (IOF). This was set up in 1961 as the main governing body of the sport worldwide. The IOF organises the world championships and has 69 nations as members.

International competitions

Every year, the best orienteers from many countries meet for the world championships. These were held in Aarhus in Denmark and Kiev in the Ukraine in 2007 and in Olomouc in the Czech Republic in 2008. There are also Junior World Championships held annually for those under 20 years old. The world orienteering championships (WOC) started up

Jamie Stevenson, one of Great Britain's elite orienteering runners, takes part in a competition.

These competitors are at the start of an orienteering relay race.

in 1966. They were originally held once every two years. However, as the sport has increased in popularity over the decades, demand has grown to hold the event more often. Since 2003 it has been held every year. There are several main competitive events – relay, sprint, middle distance and long distance.

An Olympic sport?

There has been a lot of interest in making orienteering an Olympic sport. This has not happened yet, though one day it might. In the meantime, orienteering is one of the sports included in the World Games. Like the Olympics, these games are held every four years. They are made up of sports that want to progress into the Olympic Games one day.

Glossary

Back bearing   A normal bearing taken on a compass, points the way you want to go. A back bearing points back along the route you have taken. It is 180 degrees from your original bearing.

Bearing   A reading in degrees, taken from a compass and used as a line of direction in which to travel. Bearings are always between 1 and 360 degrees.

Brikke   An electronic device that is carried by orienteers. The device is scanned over the control point to keep a record of the checkpoints that the orienteer has been to. Competitors must pass through each checkpoint.

Contour lines   Lines drawn on a map that show areas of equal height above sea level. Most orienteering maps have 5-metre or 2.5-metre height differences between each contour line.

Control point   A place on a course that competitors will have to find. Control points are marked by red and white triangles and they have a scanner through which orienteers pass their brikke.

Dehydration   Having too little water inside your body. Mild dehydration will affect how well you can think and run. Severe dehydration is very serious. Make sure you drink plenty of water or better still, isotonic drinks.

Grid lines   Lines found on a map that start at the bottom (south) and go to the top (north). They run parallel to each other. They can be used in conjunction with a compass to help you navigate.

Hypothermia   A very dangerous condition in which your body becomes too cold due to exposure to wind, rain and cool temperatures. If your core body temperature drops too low, you will need expert medical help. Good clothing and plenty of food are simple measures to prevent this condition from happening.

Leg   A word used by orienteers to describe a short part of a navigational journey from one control point to another. A leg might be from one feature (say a path junction) to another (a stream). Breaking a longer section of navigation up into smaller legs is one way of making sure you do not get lost.

Magnetic north   A place on the surface of the Earth, in the northern hemisphere, to which all magnetic needles point.

Master map   A map provided by the organisers of an orienteering competition that contains all the information needed by each competitor to complete the course.

Moorland   Land that is generally found in remote upland regions of the United Kingdom. It is used for harder orienteering events as it has few landmarks and is difficult to navigate.

Navigation   The skill of using a map and compass to find your way over an unknown region of land.

Outcrop   A word used to describe a small cliff or rock face found in a landscape.

Relocate   This is the navigational skill of being able to find yourself if lost, using features in the landscape and your map and compass.

Scale   This is the mathematical solution to putting a very large landscape onto a very small map accurately. All the features, including distances, are scaled down by the same amount to fit onto the map. For example, using the scale of 1:10 000, everything shown as a centimetre on the map would measure 100 metres in the real world.

Tendons   Special fibres found in our bodies that attach our muscles to our bones.

Terrain   The type of land.

Thermal   Clothing materials that keep you warm. They do this by trapping the heat in their fibres. Wool is a natural fibre that is thermal.

Work rate   The measure of how hard you have to work your muscles in order to achieve a goal. This might mean running hard to win a competition. The higher the work rate, the more you will sweat and the more energy you will use.

Visibility   Being able to see. Visibility is often poor when the weather is misty or foggy.

Further infomation

Books to read

Orienteering Ian Bratt, Stackpole Books (2002)

Orienteering Made Simple, An Instructional Handbook Nancy Kelly, AuthorHouse (2004)

Radical Sports: Orienteering Neil Champion, Heinemann Library (1999)

The Great Outdoors: Orienteering Joanne Mattern, Capstone Press (2004)

Walking and Orienteering Peter G Drake, Southwater (2005)

Useful contacts

The International Orienteering Federation www.orienteering.org

Orienteering Australia www.orienteering.asn.au

The British Orienteering Federation www.britishorienteering.org

The Canadian Orienteering Federation www.orienteering.ca

The *US Orienteering Federation* www.us.orienteering.org

Websites

This website offers lots of information for orienteers with disabilities: www.trailO.org

For everything you need to read to keep up to date with developments in the sport: www.orienteeringtoday.com

This useful website has all the information you could need on MTB-O: www.trailquest.co.uk/news.php

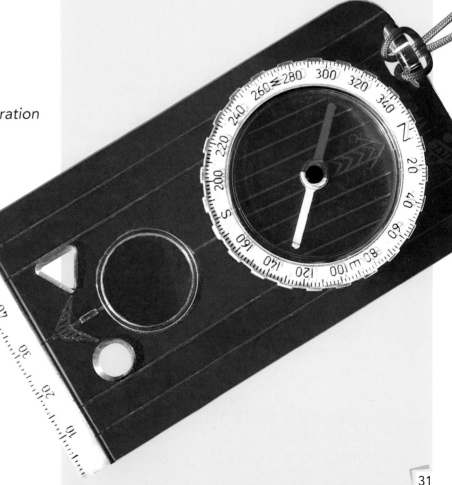

index